READ THE CONSTITUTION IN 30 DAYS!

A DAILY DEVOTIONAL FOR READING THE CONSTITUTION

BY PAUL ENGEL

Paul Engel
The Constitution Study
344 Virgil Crowell Road
Unionville, TN 37180

http://constitutionstudy.com

Every member of the State ought diligently to read and to study the constitution of his country, and teach the rising generation to be free. By knowing their rights, they will sooner perceive when they are violated, and be the better prepared to defend and assert them.

John Jay, First Chief Justice of the supreme Court of the United States

PROLOGUE

I've heard many reasons why people do not study the Constitution of the United States. "It's too hard." "I'm not a lawyer." "I don't like reading old English." And probably the saddest of them all, "The Constitution doesn't matter anymore." I know, I used to say the same things until I read it for myself.

Of course, that doesn't change the fact that the vast majority of Americans haven't read the supreme law of the land. Worse, much of what they've been taught about it is wrong. So what is a person to do? I wrote a book titled *The Constitution Study* to help everyday Americans read and study this most important of American documents, but I realized that this, too, may be too big of a bite for some people to chew.

I know that at about 8,000 words, the Constitution is not that long a document; the average person can read it I about 20 minutes. So why do so many people who seem interested in the Constitution not read it?

Maybe what people need is a simple tool to help them start. Thinking along that line, I considered how many devotionals I've read over the years. They're nice because they usually allow you to engage with a subject in small, manageable bites, usually in just a few minutes once or twice a day. So I decided to create this "devotional" for the U.S. Constitution. Each day there is a short section of the Constitution to read, followed by a short commentary on what you just read. Follow this plan every day, and in 30 days you've read the entire Constitution. Do it again, with a little more time and attention on the ideas in that day's text, and you've started studying the Constitution. More importantly, you will have taken an important step in becoming both a constitutional scholar and a better informed citizen of this great republic.

1.
THE UNANIMOUS DECLARATION

The unanimous Declaration of the thirteen united States of America, *When in the Course of human events, it becomes necessary for one people to dissolve the political bands which have connected them with another, and to assume among the powers of the earth, the separate and equal station to which the Laws of Nature and of Nature's God entitle them, a decent respect to the opinions of mankind requires that they should declare the causes which impel them to the separation.*

We hold these truths to be self-evident, that all men are created equal, that they are endowed by their Creator with certain unalienable Rights, that among these are Life, Liberty and the pursuit of Happiness.--That to secure these rights, Governments are instituted among Men, deriving their just powers from the consent of the governed, --That whenever any Form of Government becomes destructive of these ends, it is the Right of the People to alter or to abolish it, and to institute new Government, laying its foundation on such principles and organizing its powers in such form, as to them shall seem most likely to effect their Safety and Happiness. Prudence, indeed, will dictate that Governments long established should not be changed for light and transient causes; and accordingly all experience hath shewn, that mankind are more disposed to suffer, while evils are sufferable, than to right themselves by abolishing the forms to which they are accustomed. But when a long train of abuses and usurpations, pursuing invariably the same Object evinces a design to reduce them under absolute Despotism, it is their right, it is their duty, to throw off such Government, and to provide new Guards for their future security.--Such has been the patient sufferance of these Colonies; and such is now the necessity which constrains them to alter their former Systems of Government. The history of the present King of Great Britain is a history of repeated injuries and usurpations, all having in direct object the establishment of an absolute Tyranny over these States. To prove this, let Facts be submitted to a candid world.

THE UNANIMOUS DECLARATION OF THE THIRTEEN UNITED STATES OF AMERICA

When we declared independence, our Founding Fathers did not create a single nation, but thirteen free and independent states. Only later would these states join together into the union we know of as the United States of America. With this document, our founders not only declared they were independent of Great Britain, but why.

Some of the most famous words in American history exist in the second paragraph. "We hold these truths to be self-evident, that all men are created equal, that they are endowed by their Creator with certain unalienable Rights, that among these are Life, Liberty and the pursuit of Happiness." Only slightly less important are the words that follow: "That to secure these rights, Governments are instituted among Men, deriving their just powers from the consent of the governed". Governments are created with the primary purpose of protecting our rights. And they get their just powers from our consent, whether it be active or passive. Remember that the next time you walk into a voting booth.

2.
GRIEVANCES

The history of the present King of Great Britain is a history of repeated injuries and usurpations, all having in direct object the establishment of an absolute Tyranny over these States. To prove this, let Facts be submitted to a candid world.

He has refused his Assent to Laws, the most wholesome and necessary for the public good.

He has forbidden his Governors to pass Laws of immediate and pressing importance, unless suspended in their operation till his Assent should be obtained; and when so suspended, he has utterly neglected to attend to them.

He has refused to pass other Laws for the accommodation of large districts of people, unless those people would relinquish the right of Representation in the Legislature, a right inestimable to them and formidable to tyrants only.

He has called together legislative bodies at places unusual, uncomfortable, and distant from the depository of their public Records, for the sole purpose of fatiguing them into compliance with his measures.

He has dissolved Representative Houses repeatedly, for opposing with manly firmness his invasions on the rights of the people.

He has refused for a long time, after such dissolutions, to cause others to be elected; whereby the Legislative powers, incapable of Annihilation, have returned to the People at large for their exercise; the State remaining in the mean time exposed to all the dangers of invasion from without, and convulsions within.

He has endeavoured to prevent the population of these States; for that purpose obstructing the Laws for Naturalization of Foreigners; refusing to pass others to encourage their migrations hither, and raising the conditions of new Appropriations of Lands.
He has obstructed the Administration of Justice, by refusing his Assent to Laws for establishing Judiciary powers.
He has made Judges dependent on his Will alone, for the tenure of their offices, and the amount and payment of their salaries.
He has erected a multitude of New Offices, and sent hither swarms of Officers to harrass our people, and eat out their substance.
He has kept among us, in times of peace, Standing Armies without the Consent of our legislatures.

TO PROVE THIS, LET FACTS BE SUBMITTED TO A CANDID WORLD.

The Continental Congress had already passed the Lee Resolution, where they had declared that the colonies were free and independent states. So why this public declaration of what they had already done?

As the Declaration states, the colonies had been repeatedly subjected to injury and usurpation by the King of Great Britain, but what they had done could be called treason. So to prove that they were left with no other choice, they published the Declaration of Independence. They didn't just want the king to know what they were doing and why, but the entire world as well. As you read the grievances listed here and in the next chapter, think about how many could be filed against our governments in Washington, D.C. and our state capitals now.

3.
MORE GRIEVANCES

He has affected to render the Military independent of and superior to the Civil power.

He has combined with others to subject us to a jurisdiction foreign to our constitution, and unacknowledged by our laws; giving his Assent to their Acts of pretended Legislation:

For Quartering large bodies of armed troops among us:

For protecting them, by a mock Trial, from punishment for any Murders which they should commit on the Inhabitants of these States:

For cutting off our Trade with all parts of the world:

For imposing Taxes on us without our Consent:

For depriving us in many cases, of the benefits of Trial by Jury:

For transporting us beyond Seas to be tried for pretended offences

For abolishing the free System of English Laws in a neighbouring Province, establishing therein an Arbitrary government, and enlarging its Boundaries so as to render it at once an example and fit instrument for introducing the same absolute rule into these Colonies:

For taking away our Charters, abolishing our most valuable Laws, and altering fundamentally the Forms of our Governments:

For suspending our own Legislatures, and declaring themselves invested with power to legislate for us in all cases whatsoever.

He has abdicated Government here, by declaring us out of his Protection and waging War against us.

He has plundered our seas, ravaged our Coasts, burnt our towns, and destroyed the lives of our people.
He is at this time transporting large Armies of foreign Mercenaries to compleat the works of death, desolation and tyranny, already begun with circumstances of Cruelty & perfidy scarcely paralleled in the most barbarous ages, and totally unworthy the Head of a civilized nation.
He has constrained our fellow Citizens taken Captive on the high Seas to bear Arms against their Country, to become the executioners of their friends and Brethren, or to fall themselves by their Hands.
He has excited domestic insurrections amongst us, and has endeavoured to bring on the inhabitants of our frontiers, the merciless Indian Savages, whose known rule of warfare, is an undistinguished destruction of all ages, sexes and conditions.

FOR IMPOSING TAXES ON US WITHOUT OUR CONSENT

In school, I learned that the reason we declared independence was "taxation without representation". While unfair taxes was one of the grievances, it was number 17 out of 27, which is pretty low on the list for the one reason most of us were given for our independence.

So, now that you've read through the reasons we separated from Great Britain and hopefully compared our situation with that of our Founding Fathers, do you think these usurpations are still tolerable?

4.
IN THE NAME AND BY THE AUTHORITY

In every stage of these Oppressions We have Petitioned for Redress in the most humble terms: Our repeated Petitions have been answered only by repeated injury. A Prince whose character is thus marked by every act which may define a Tyrant, is unfit to be the ruler of a free people. Nor have We been wanting in attentions to our British brethren. We have warned them from time to time of attempts by their legislature to extend an unwarrantable jurisdiction over us. We have reminded them of the circumstances of our emigration and settlement here. We have appealed to their native justice and magnanimity, and we have conjured them by the ties of our common kindred to disavow these usurpations, which, would inevitably interrupt our connections and correspondence. They too have been deaf to the voice of justice and of consanguinity. We must, therefore, acquiesce in the necessity, which denounces our Separation, and hold them, as we hold the rest of mankind, Enemies in War, in Peace Friends.

We, therefore, the Representatives of the united States of America, in General Congress, Assembled, appealing to the Supreme Judge of the world for the rectitude of our intentions, do, in the Name, and by Authority of the good People of these Colonies, solemnly publish and declare, That these United Colonies are, and of Right ought to be Free and Independent States; that they are Absolved from all Allegiance to the British Crown, and that all political connection between them and the State of Great Britain, is and ought to be totally dissolved; and that as Free and Independent States, they have full Power to levy War, *conclude Peace, contract Alliances, establish Commerce, and to do all other Acts and Things which Independent States may of right do. And for the support of this Declaration, with a firm reliance on the protection of divine Providence, we mutually pledge to each other our Lives, our Fortunes and our sacred Honor.*

WE MUTUALLY PLEDGE TO EACH OTHER OUR LIVES, OUR FORTUNES AND OUR SACRED HONOR

What would you pledge for your liberty? What would you promise to give up if it meant not only that you could live free, but that your children and grand-children could as well?

Our Founding Fathers pledged to each other their very lives. Some would suffer for their actions and others would die, but they had pledged to each other their lives for the cause of liberty. Some lost everything they owned: Their farms, their businesses, their homes, and their fortunes. All for the chance to live in a free country.

For many of our Founding Fathers, nothing was more important than their honor. They were willing to pledge their honor to the cause of liberty. So I ask again, what are you willing to pledge for your own and your family's liberty? Will you take the time to read and study the Constitution? Will you learn about your rights and liberties? Will you vet the candidates for office based on their constitutional actions rather than what party they are a member of? Will you pledge the time to serve on a jury to ensure justice for others?

5.
PREAMBLE

We the People of the United States, in Order to form a more perfect Union, establish Justice, insure domestic Tranquility, provide for the common defence, promote the general Welfare, and secure the Blessings of Liberty to ourselves and our Posterity, do ordain and establish this Constitution for the United States of America.

SECURE THE BLESSINGS OF LIBERTY TO OURSELVES AND OUR POSTERITY

While today's quote is short, it is packed with pathos and meaning. The preamble is not legally binding, but it does explain what our Founding Fathers were trying to do when they wrote the Constitution.

After the Declaration of Independence, the newly born states formed a union called the United States of America under the Articles of Confederation. The Articles had issues though, not the least of which was lacking any ability to amend them.

Our founders wanted to make the union better and they wanted to establish justice. Just look at how many grievances revolved around justice. The king interfering with the creations of laws, placing the military above the law, conscripting citizens, and declaring the colonies out of his protection. How many of the grievances dealt with the judicial system?]He subjected citizens to foreign jurisdictions, deprived many of a trial by jury, transported the accused overseas for trial, and even abolished English laws.

Our founders also wanted to insure domestic tranquility, provide for a common defense, and promote the general welfare. (I talk more about the General Welfare Clause on my website.) Still, the most important reason our founders created the Constitution was to secure the blessings of liberty, both for themselves and for those who followed them. That's right, one of the main reasons we have a Constitution for the United States of America is to secure the blessings of liberty for you and for your children. That is also why it is so important that everyone read and study the Constitution for themselves. That way we know how to assert our rights, and gain the blessings of liberty that comes with doing so. When government is not protecting our rights and not securing the blessings of liberty for us, we know how to defend those blessings. And not just for ourselves or our children, but for our neighbors and fellow citizens as well.

6.
HOUSE OF REPRESENTATIVES

Article I
Section. 1.
All legislative Powers herein granted shall be vested in a Congress of the United States, which shall consist of a Senate and House of Representatives.
Section. 2.
The House of Representatives shall be composed of Members chosen every second Year by the People of the several States, and the Electors in each State shall have the Qualifications requisite for Electors of the most numerous Branch of the State Legislature.
No Person shall be a Representative who shall not have attained to the Age of twenty five Years, and been seven Years a Citizen of the United States, and who shall not, when elected, be an Inhabitant of that State in which he shall be chosen.
Representatives and direct Taxes shall be apportioned among the several States which may be included within this Union, according to their respective Numbers, which shall be determined by adding to the whole Number of free Persons, including those bound to Service for a Term of Years, and excluding Indians not taxed, three fifths of all other Persons. The actual Enumeration shall be made within three Years after the first Meeting of the Congress of the United States, and within every subsequent Term of ten Years, in such Manner as they shall by Law direct. The Number of Representatives shall not exceed one for every thirty Thousand, but each State shall have at Least one Representative; and until such enumeration shall be made,

the State of New Hampshire shall be entitled to chuse three, Massachusetts eight, Rhode-Island and Providence Plantations one, Connecticut five, New-York six, New Jersey four, Pennsylvania eight, Delaware one, Maryland six, Virginia ten, North Carolina five, South Carolina five, and Georgia three.

When vacancies happen in the Representation from any State, the Executive Authority thereof shall issue Writs of Election to fill such Vacancies.

The House of Representatives shall chuse their Speaker and other Officers; and shall have the sole Power of Impeachment.

THE HOUSE OF REPRESENTATIVES SHALL BE COMPOSED OF MEMBERS CHOSEN EVERY SECOND YEAR BY THE PEOPLE OF THE SEVERAL STATES,

The House of Representatives is sometimes referred to as the people's house, because that is its purpose. That means that everyone elected to a seat in the House is there to represent the people of their district. Not the states, not the federal government, and not the political parties. The people. As we learn more about this house, keep in mind that the powers delegated to it are for your representatives.

7.
SENATE

*Article I
Section. 3.
The Senate of the United States shall be composed of two Senators from each State, chosen by the Legislature thereof, for six Years; and each Senator shall have one Vote. Immediately after they shall be assembled in Consequence of the first Election, they shall be divided as equally as may be into three Classes. The Seats of the Senators of the first Class shall be vacated at the Expiration of the second Year, of the second Class at the Expiration of the fourth Year, and of the third Class at the Expiration of the sixth Year, so that one third may be chosen every second Year; and if Vacancies happen by Resignation, or otherwise, during the Recess of the Legislature of any State, the Executive thereof may make temporary Appointments until the next Meeting of the Legislature, which shall then fill such Vacancies.
No Person shall be a Senator who shall not have attained to the Age of thirty Years, and been nine Years a Citizen of the United States, and who shall not, when elected, be an Inhabitant of that State for which he shall be chosen.
The Vice President of the United States shall be President of the Senate, but shall have no Vote, unless they be equally divided.
The Senate shall chuse their other Officers, and also a President pro tempore, in the Absence of the Vice President, or when he shall exercise the Office of President of the United States.
The Senate shall have the sole Power to try all Impeachments. When sitting for that Purpose, they shall be*

on Oath or Affirmation. When the President of the United States is tried, the Chief Justice shall preside: And no Person shall be convicted without the Concurrence of two thirds of the Members present.

Judgment in Cases of Impeachment shall not extend further than to removal from Office, and disqualification to hold and enjoy any Office of honor, Trust or Profit under the United States: but the Party convicted shall nevertheless be liable and subject to Indictment, Trial, Judgment and Punishment, according to Law.

Section. 4.

The Times, Places and Manner of holding Elections for Senators and Representatives, shall be prescribed in each State by the Legislature thereof; but the Congress may at any time by Law make or alter such Regulations, except as to the Places of chusing Senators.

The Congress shall assemble at least once in every Year, and such Meeting shall be on the first Monday in December, unless they shall by Law appoint a different Day.

THE SENATE OF THE UNITED STATES SHALL BE COMPOSED OF TWO SENATORS FROM EACH STATE

While sometimes referred to as the "upper house", the Senate consists of the representatives of the states. While the method of electing Senators was changed with the 17th Amendment, their role and responsibility to represent the states has not changed. Keep that in mind as we learn about the powers delegated to the Senate.

8.
RULES FOR CONGRESS

Article I
Section. 5.
Each House shall be the Judge of the Elections, Returns and Qualifications of its own Members, and a Majority of each shall constitute a Quorum to do Business; but a smaller Number may adjourn from day to day, and may be authorized to compel the Attendance of absent Members, in such Manner, and under such Penalties as each House may provide.

Each House may determine the Rules of its Proceedings, punish its Members for disorderly Behaviour, and, with the Concurrence of two thirds, expel a Member.

Each House shall keep a Journal of its Proceedings, and from time to time publish the same, excepting such Parts as may in their Judgment require Secrecy; and the Yeas and Nays of the Members of either House on any question shall, at the Desire of one fifth of those Present, be entered on the Journal.

Neither House, during the Session of Congress, shall, without the Consent of the other, adjourn for more than three days, nor to any other Place than that in which the two Houses shall be sitting.

Section. 6.
The Senators and Representatives shall receive a Compensation for their Services, to be ascertained by Law, and paid out of the Treasury of the United States. They shall in all Cases, except Treason, Felony and Breach of the Peace, be privileged from Arrest during their Attendance at the Session of their respective Houses, and in going to and

returning from the same; and for any Speech or Debate in either House, they shall not be questioned in any other Place. No Senator or Representative shall, during the Time for which he was elected, be appointed to any civil Office under the Authority of the United States, which shall have been created, or the Emoluments whereof shall have been encreased during such time; and no Person holding any Office under the United States, shall be a Member of either House during his Continuance in Office.

EACH HOUSE MAY DETERMINE THE RULES OF ITS PROCEEDINGS, PUNISH ITS MEMBERS FOR DISORDERLY BEHAVIOUR

This section focuses on rules for Congress. Each House has the authority to determine the rules for their proceedings. They must also keep a journal of those proceedings. Have you ever asked yourself why? The answer is so the people can oversee the people they hire to represent them and their states. Congress, with rare exception, should be doing nothing in secret. The American people should be holding their elected agents accountable for what they are doing and what they are not doing.

9.
PASSING LEGISLATION

*Article I
Section. 7.
All Bills for raising Revenue shall originate in the House of Representatives; but the Senate may propose or concur with Amendments as on other Bills.
Every Bill which shall have passed the House of Representatives and the Senate, shall, before it become a Law, be presented to the President of the United States; If he approve he shall sign it, but if not he shall return it, with his Objections to that House in which it shall have originated, who shall enter the Objections at large on their Journal, and proceed to reconsider it. If after such Reconsideration two thirds of that House shall agree to pass the Bill, it shall be sent, together with the Objections, to the other House, by which it shall likewise be reconsidered, and if approved by two thirds of that House, it shall become a Law. But in all such Cases the Votes of both Houses shall be determined by yeas and Nays, and the Names of the Persons voting for and against the Bill shall be entered on the Journal of each House respectively. If any Bill shall not be returned by the President within ten Days (Sundays excepted) after it shall have been presented to him, the Same shall be a Law, in like Manner as if he had signed it, unless the Congress by their Adjournment prevent its Return, in which Case it shall not be a Law.
Every Order, Resolution, or Vote to which the Concurrence of the Senate and House of Representatives may be necessary (except on a question of Adjournment) shall be presented to*

ALL BILLS FOR RAISING REVENUE SHALL ORIGINATE IN THE HOUSE OF REPRESENTATIVES;

Why are all bills for raising revenue (taxes) required to originate in the House of Representatives? Because it is the representatives of the people who hold the power of the purse. That's right, your representatives in Congress hold the purse strings. So if those in the executive branch violate their oaths to support the Constitution, it is your representatives that can defund them. If an executive agency enacts an unconstitutional program, your representatives can defund it. If an executive agency acts beyond its commission, your representatives can cut off its life's blood. And if the President sends troops overseas beyond his authority, Congress can cut off the money for it.

People often talk about the President as "the most powerful person in the free world." The President, however, can do little without the funding to enact his policies. The vast majority of the powers delegated to the United States belong to Congress. And of those powers, few rival the effectiveness of the power of the purse.

10.
POWERS OF CONGRESS

Article I
Section. 8.
The Congress shall have Power To lay and collect Taxes, Duties, Imposts and Excises, to pay the Debts and provide for the common Defence and general Welfare of the United States; but all Duties, Imposts and Excises shall be uniform throughout the United States;
To borrow Money on the credit of the United States;
To regulate Commerce with foreign Nations, and among the several States, and with the Indian Tribes;
To establish an uniform Rule of Naturalization, and uniform Laws on the subject of Bankruptcies throughout the United States;
To coin Money, regulate the Value thereof, and of foreign Coin, and fix the Standard of Weights and Measures;
To provide for the Punishment of counterfeiting the Securities and current Coin of the United States;
To establish Post Offices and post Roads;
To promote the Progress of Science and useful Arts, by securing for limited Times to Authors and Inventors the exclusive Right to their respective Writings and Discoveries;
To constitute Tribunals inferior to the supreme Court;
To define and punish Piracies and Felonies committed on the high Seas, and Offences against the Law of Nations;
To declare War, grant Letters of Marque and Reprisal, and make Rules concerning Captures on Land and Water;
To raise and support Armies, but no Appropriation of Money to that Use shall be for a longer Term than two Years;
To provide and maintain a Navy;

To make Rules for the Government and Regulation of the land and naval Forces;

To provide for calling forth the Militia to execute the Laws of the Union, suppress Insurrections and repel Invasions;

To provide for organizing, arming, and disciplining, the Militia, and for governing such Part of them as may be employed in the Service of the United States, reserving to the States respectively, the Appointment of the Officers, and the Authority of training the Militia according to the discipline prescribed by Congress;

To exercise exclusive Legislation in all Cases whatsoever, over such District (not exceeding ten Miles square) as may, by Cession of particular States, and the Acceptance of Congress, become the Seat of the Government of the United States, and to exercise like Authority over all Places purchased by the Consent of the Legislature of the State in which the Same shall be, for the Erection of Forts, Magazines, Arsenals, dock-Yards, and other needful Buildings;—And

To make all Laws which shall be necessary and proper for carrying into Execution the foregoing Powers, and all other Powers vested by this Constitution in the Government of the United States, or in any Department or Officer thereof.

THE CONGRESS SHALL HAVE POWER TO LAY AND COLLECT TAXES,

Section 8 lists most of the powers delegated to Congress. While most people complain about the IRS on April 15th, it is Congress that determines what taxes are collected and how they are spent. Few Americans seem aware the Congress is limited in what they can legally collect taxes for, so they spend our money illegally and the people do nothing about it.

11.
LIMITATIONS ON CONGRESS & STATES

rticle I
Section. 9.
The Migration or Importation of such Persons as any of the States now existing shall think proper to admit, shall not be prohibited by the Congress prior to the Year one thousand eight hundred and eight, but a Tax or duty may be imposed on such Importation, not exceeding ten dollars for each Person.

The Privilege of the Writ of Habeas Corpus shall not be suspended, unless when in Cases of Rebellion or Invasion the public Safety may require it.

No Bill of Attainder or ex post facto Law shall be passed.

No Capitation, or other direct, Tax shall be laid, unless in Proportion to the Census or enumeration herein before directed to be taken.

No Tax or Duty shall be laid on Articles exported from any State.

No Preference shall be given by any Regulation of Commerce or Revenue to the Ports of one State over those of another: nor shall Vessels bound to, or from, one State, be obliged to enter, clear, or pay Duties in another.

No Money shall be drawn from the Treasury, but in Consequence of Appropriations made by Law; and a regular Statement and Account of the Receipts and Expenditures of all public Money shall be published from time to time.

No Title of Nobility shall be granted by the United States: And no Person holding any Office of Profit or Trust under them, shall, without the Consent of the Congress, accept of any present, Emolument, Office, or Title, of any kind whatever, from any King, Prince, or foreign State.

Section. 10.

No State shall enter into any Treaty, Alliance, or Confederation; grant Letters of Marque and Reprisal; coin Money; emit Bills of Credit; make any Thing but gold and silver Coin a Tender in Payment of Debts; pass any Bill of Attainder, ex post facto Law, or Law impairing the Obligation of Contracts, or grant any Title of Nobility.

No State shall, without the Consent of the Congress, lay any Imposts or Duties on Imports or Exports, except what may be absolutely necessary for executing it's inspection Laws: and the net Produce of all Duties and Imposts, laid by any State on Imports or Exports, shall be for the Use of the Treasury of the United States; and all such Laws shall be subject to the Revision and Controul of the Congress.

No State shall, without the Consent of Congress, lay any Duty of Tonnage, keep Troops, or Ships of War in time of Peace, enter into any Agreement or Compact with another State, or with a foreign Power, or engage in War, unless actually invaded, or in such imminent Danger as will not admit of delay.

NO CAPITATION, OR OTHER DIRECT, TAX SHALL BE LAID, UNLESS IN PROPORTION TO THE CENSUS

Within the powers delegated to Congress, and those reserved to the states, are limitations. One of the most powerful was from where Congress could collect taxes. That worked until the <u>16th Amendment</u> was ratified.

12.
THE PRESIDENT

Article II
Section. 1.
The executive Power shall be vested in a President of the United States of America. He shall hold his Office during the Term of four Years, and, together with the Vice President, chosen for the same Term, be elected, as follows
Each State shall appoint, in such Manner as the Legislature thereof may direct, a Number of Electors, equal to the whole Number of Senators and Representatives to which the State may be entitled in the Congress: but no Senator or Representative, or Person holding an Office of Trust or Profit under the United States, shall be appointed an Elector.
The Electors shall meet in their respective States, and vote by Ballot for two Persons, of whom one at least shall not be an Inhabitant of the same State with themselves. And they shall make a List of all the Persons voted for, and of the Number of Votes for each; which List they shall sign and certify, and transmit sealed to the Seat of the Government of the United States, directed to the President of the Senate. The President of the Senate shall, in the Presence of the Senate and House of Representatives, open all the Certificates, and the Votes shall then be counted. The Person having the greatest Number of Votes shall be the President, if such Number be a Majority of the whole Number of Electors appointed; and if there be more than one who have such Majority, and have an equal Number of Votes, then the House of Representatives shall immediately chuse by Ballot one of them for President; and if no Person have a Majority, then from the five highest on the List the said House shall in

like Manner chuse the President. But in chusing the President, the Votes shall be taken by States, the Representation from each State having one Vote; A quorum for this Purpose shall consist of a Member or Members from two thirds of the States, and a Majority of all the States shall be necessary to a Choice. In every Case, after the Choice of the President, the Person having the greatest Number of Votes of the Electors shall be the Vice President. But if there should remain two or more who have equal Votes, the Senate shall chuse from them by Ballot the Vice President.

EACH STATE SHALL APPOINT, IN SUCH MANNER AS THE LEGISLATURE THEREOF MAY DIRECT, A NUMBER OF ELECTORS

If there is one thing that most Americans do not understand about our Presidential elections, it's that the people do not elect the President. Here Clause 2 says the states appoint electors, not that the people elect them. And that the method of appointing electors is up to the legislature of the state. That is why, if you look closely at your ballot, you'll see that you are voting for electors for a candidate. They are still appointed, but the state legislature has decided to do so based on a popular state election.

These anonymous electors have pledged to vote for a certain candidate for President. In most states, it is illegal for them to not vote for their pledged candidate should they be appointed. Some states even impose fines for these "faithless electors". So the next time you don't like the way your state's electors are appointed, blame your state's legislators.

13.
THE PRESIDENT CONT'D

*rticle II
Section. 1 (cont'd).
The Congress may determine the Time of chusing the Electors, and the Day on which they shall give their Votes; which Day shall be the same throughout the United States. No Person except a natural born Citizen, or a Citizen of the United States, at the time of the Adoption of this Constitution, shall be eligible to the Office of President; neither shall any Person be eligible to that Office who shall not have attained to the Age of thirty five Years, and been fourteen Years a Resident within the United States.*

In Case of the Removal of the President from Office, or of his Death, Resignation, or Inability to discharge the Powers and Duties of the said Office, the Same shall devolve on the Vice President, and the Congress may by Law provide for the Case of Removal, Death, Resignation or Inability, both of the President and Vice President, declaring what Officer shall then act as President, and such Officer shall act accordingly, until the Disability be removed, or a President shall be elected.

The President shall, at stated Times, receive for his Services, a Compensation, which shall neither be encreased nor diminished during the Period for which he shall have been elected, and he shall not receive within that Period any other Emolument from the United States, or any of them.

Before he enter on the Execution of his Office, he shall take the following Oath or Affirmation:—"I do solemnly swear (or affirm) that I will faithfully execute the Office of President of

NO PERSON EXCEPT A NATURAL BORN CITIZEN, OR A CITIZEN OF THE UNITED STATES, AT THE TIME OF THE ADOPTION OF THIS CONSTITUTION, SHALL BE ELIGIBLE TO THE OFFICE OF PRESIDENT;

What is a natural born citizen? While I've read several articles and papers with different claims and assertions, the simple answer is someone born a citizen. The Constitution delegated to Congress the power to make a uniform rule of naturalization (Article I, Section 8, Clause 4), which states that if you are born to at least one U.S. citizen, you are eligible to be a natural born citizen. If you were born on U.S. soil, you are automatically a citizen. If you are born on foreign soil, then your parents must apply to the U.S. diplomatic service for recognition of your citizenship.

Why must the President be a natural born citizen? No other federal office makes such a requirement. Because, unlike any other office created by the Constitution, the executive power of the United States is invested in a single person: The President. Since the idea of America is so unique in the world, our founders did not want someone unfamiliar with our history and traditions to hold such an office alone.

14.
COMMANDER IN CHIEF

Article II
Section. 2.
The President shall be Commander in Chief of the Army and Navy of the United States, and of the Militia of the several States, when called into the actual Service of the United States; he may require the Opinion, in writing, of the principal Officer in each of the executive Departments, upon any Subject relating to the Duties of their respective Offices, and he shall have Power to grant Reprieves and Pardons for Offences against the United States, except in Cases of Impeachment.

He shall have Power, by and with the Advice and Consent of the Senate, to make Treaties, provided two thirds of the Senators present concur; and he shall nominate, and by and with the Advice and Consent of the Senate, shall appoint Ambassadors, other public Ministers and Consuls, Judges of the supreme Court, and all other Officers of the United States, whose Appointments are not herein otherwise provided for, and which shall be established by Law: but the Congress may by Law vest the Appointment of such inferior Officers, as they think proper, in the President alone, in the Courts of Law, or in the Heads of Departments.

The President shall have Power to fill up all Vacancies that may happen during the Recess of the Senate, by granting Commissions which shall expire at the End of their next Session.

Section. 3.
He shall from time to time give to the Congress Information of the State of the Union, and recommend to their

THE PRESIDENT SHALL BE COMMANDER IN CHIEF OF THE ARMY AND NAVY OF THE UNITED STATES

A lot is made of the fact that the President is the Commander in Chief of the military. Often lost is the boundaries placed around such power.

Congress has been delegated the power to declare war, (Article I, Section 8, Clauses 11) and to raise and support the military (Clauses 12 and 13). They have also been delegated the power to regulate the military (Clause 14). So while the President is Commander in Chief, it is Congress who establishes the rules under which he must act.

15.
THE COURTS

A rticle III
Section. 1.
The judicial Power of the United States, shall be vested in one supreme Court, and in such inferior Courts as the Congress may from time to time ordain and establish. The Judges, both of the supreme and inferior Courts, shall hold their Offices during good Behaviour, and shall, at stated Times, receive for their Services, a Compensation, which shall not be diminished during their Continuance in Office.
Section. 2.
The judicial Power shall extend to all Cases, in Law and Equity, arising under this Constitution, the Laws of the United States, and Treaties made, or which shall be made, under their Authority;—to all Cases affecting Ambassadors, other public Ministers and Consuls;—to all Cases of admiralty and maritime Jurisdiction;—to Controversies to which the United States shall be a Party;—to Controversies between two or more States;— between a State and Citizens of another State,—between Citizens of different States,—between Citizens of the same State claiming Lands under Grants of different States, and between a State, or the Citizens thereof, and foreign States, Citizens or Subjects.
In all Cases affecting Ambassadors, other public Ministers and Consuls, and those in which a State shall be Party, the supreme Court shall have original Jurisdiction. In all the other Cases before mentioned, the supreme Court shall have appellate Jurisdiction, both as to Law and Fact, with such Exceptions, and under such Regulations as the Congress shall make.

The Trial of all Crimes, except in Cases of Impeachment, shall be by Jury; and such Trial shall be held in the State where the said Crimes shall have been committed; but when not committed within any State, the Trial shall be at such Place or Places as the Congress may by Law have directed.
Section. 3.
Treason against the United States, shall consist only in levying War against them, or in adhering to their Enemies, giving them Aid and Comfort. No Person shall be convicted of Treason unless on the Testimony of two Witnesses to the same overt Act, or on Confession in open Court.
The Congress shall have Power to declare the Punishment of Treason, but no Attainder of Treason shall work Corruption of Blood, or Forfeiture except during the Life of the Person attainted.

SHALL BE VESTED IN ONE SUPREME COURT, AND IN SUCH INFERIOR COURTS AS THE CONGRESS MAY FROM TIME TO TIME ORDAIN AND ESTABLISH.

Today, the judges in federal courts are treated as the supreme arbiters of just about everything, but we see here that most of the federal courts are actually the creations of Congress. We also see that federal judges do not receive lifetime appointments, but can only hold their office during good behavior, which means that the jurisdiction of the federal courts is rather limited. So why do most Americans genuflect before the opinions of these black robed high priests? I believe it's because most of them have never read the Constitution and don't know what it says.

16.
THE CENTRAL GOVERNMENT

Article IV
Section. 1.
Full Faith and Credit shall be given in each State to the public Acts, Records, and judicial Proceedings of every other State. And the Congress may by general Laws prescribe the Manner in which such Acts, Records and Proceedings shall be proved, and the Effect thereof.
Section. 2.
The Citizens of each State shall be entitled to all Privileges and Immunities of Citizens in the several States.
A Person charged in any State with Treason, Felony, or other Crime, who shall flee from Justice, and be found in another State, shall on Demand of the executive Authority of the State from which he fled, be delivered up, to be removed to the State having Jurisdiction of the Crime.
No Person held to Service or Labour in one State, under the Laws thereof, escaping into another, shall, in Consequence of any Law or Regulation therein, be discharged from such Service or Labour, but shall be delivered up on Claim of the Party to whom such Service or Labour may be due.
Section. 3.
New States may be admitted by the Congress into this Union; but no new State shall be formed or erected within the Jurisdiction of any other State; nor any State be formed by the Junction of two or more States, or Parts of States, without the Consent of the Legislatures of the States concerned as well as of the Congress.
The Congress shall have Power to dispose of and make all needful Rules and Regulations respecting the Territory or

FULL FAITH AND CREDIT SHALL BE GIVEN IN EACH STATE TO THE PUBLIC ACTS, RECORDS, AND JUDICIAL PROCEEDINGS OF EVERY OTHER STATE.

Most people think of themselves as citizens of one nation, as the Pledge of Allegiance says, but we are actually citizens of our own state first and foremost. As a union of states, the Constitution was designed to insure that the citizens of those states are all treated equally. One of the reasons your driver's license is accepted in all fifty states is because of the Full Faith and Credit Clause of the Constitution. However, many states have decided to limit that credit only to the public acts, records, and proceedings with which they agree. So what happens when the citizens of one state are not treated the same as those from another? Today, that issue tends to be ignored.

17.
SUPREME LAW

Article. V.
The Congress, whenever two thirds of both Houses shall deem it necessary, shall propose Amendments to this Constitution, or, on the Application of the Legislatures of two thirds of the several States, shall call a Convention for proposing Amendments, which, in either Case, shall be valid to all Intents and Purposes, as Part of this Constitution, when ratified by the Legislatures of three fourths of the several States, or by Conventions in three fourths thereof, as the one or the other Mode of Ratification may be proposed by the Congress; Provided that no Amendment which may be made prior to the Year One thousand eight hundred and eight shall in any Manner affect the first and fourth Clauses in the Ninth Section of the first Article; and that no State, without its Consent, shall be deprived of its equal Suffrage in the Senate.

Article. VI.
All Debts contracted and Engagements entered into, before the Adoption of this Constitution, shall be as valid against the United States under this Constitution, as under the Confederation.

This Constitution, and the Laws of the United States which shall be made in Pursuance thereof; and all Treaties made, or which shall be made, under the Authority of the United States, shall be the supreme Law of the Land; and the Judges in every State shall be bound thereby, any Thing in the Constitution or Laws of any State to the Contrary notwithstanding.

THIS CONSTITUTION,... SHALL BE THE SUPREME LAW OF THE LAND;

I hear a lot of people complain that certain things are unconstitutional. Rarely though, do I hear those same problems referred to as illegal. As the supreme law of the land, anything that violates the Constitution is a violation of the law. That also means that when a citizen peacefully refuses to comply with an illegal law or order, they are not breaking the law but upholding it. Shouldn't the citizens of this country hold their elected officials at all levels, federal, state, and local, to their oath to support the Constitution? When a public official is caught breaking the law, there are calls for his or her removal. So why not when they are caught breaking the supreme law of the land?

18.
THE BILL OF RIGHTS

THE Conventions of a number of the States, having at the time of their adopting the Constitution, expressed a desire, in order to prevent misconstruction or abuse of its powers, that further declaratory and restrictive clauses should be added: And as extending the ground of public confidence in the Government, will best ensure the beneficent ends of its institution.

RESOLVED by the Senate and House of Representatives of the United States of America, in Congress assembled, two thirds of both Houses concurring, that the following Articles be proposed to the Legislatures of the several States, as amendments to the Constitution of the United States, all, or any of which Articles, when ratified by three fourths of the said Legislatures, to be valid to all intents and purposes, as part of the said Constitution; viz.

ARTICLES in addition to, and Amendment of the Constitution of the United States of America, proposed by Congress, and ratified by the Legislatures of the several States, pursuant to the fifth Article of the original Constitution.

Amendment I

Congress shall make no law respecting an establishment of religion, or prohibiting the free exercise thereof; or abridging the freedom of speech, or of the press; or the right of the people peaceably to assemble, and to petition the Government for a redress of grievances.

Amendment II

A well regulated Militia, being necessary to the security of a free State, the right of the people to keep and bear Arms, shall not be infringed.

Amendment III
No Soldier shall, in time of peace be quartered in any house, without the consent of the Owner, nor in time of war, but in a manner to be prescribed by law.
Amendment IV
The right of the people to be secure in their persons, houses, papers, and effects, against unreasonable searches and seizures, shall not be violated, and no Warrants shall issue, but upon probable cause, supported by Oath or affirmation, and particularly describing the place to be searched, and the persons or things to be seized.

THAT FURTHER DECLARATORY AND RESTRICTIVE CLAUSES SHOULD BE ADDED:

The road to ratification for the Constitution was not a smooth one. Several states refused to ratify it since it did not include protections for the rights of individuals. There was also some debate around the need for a Bill of Rights.

The compromise that ended up saving the Constitution was the willingness of states to qualify their ratification with the requirement that the first Congress propose a Bill of Rights as amendments to it. These first ten amendments are specific declaratory clauses meant to restrict the powers of governments, and only the governments, in the new union.

19.
THE BILL OF RIGHTS CONT'D

Amendment V
No person shall be held to answer for a capital, or otherwise infamous crime, unless on a presentment or indictment of a Grand Jury, except in cases arising in the land or naval forces, or in the Militia, when in actual service in time of War or public danger; nor shall any person be subject for the same offence to be twice put in jeopardy of life or limb; nor shall be compelled in any criminal case to be a witness against himself, nor be deprived of life, liberty, or property, without due process of law; nor shall private property be taken for public use, without just compensation.

Amendment VI
In all criminal prosecutions, the accused shall enjoy the right to a speedy and public trial, by an impartial jury of the State and district wherein the crime shall have been committed, which district shall have been previously ascertained by law, and to be informed of the nature and cause of the accusation; to be confronted with the witnesses against him; to have compulsory process for obtaining witnesses in his favor, and to have the Assistance of Counsel for his defence.

Amendment VII
In Suits at common law, where the value in controversy shall exceed twenty dollars, the right of trial by jury shall be preserved, and no fact tried by a jury, shall be otherwise re-examined in any Court of the United States, than according to the rules of the common law.

Amendment VIII
Excessive bail shall not be required, nor excessive fines imposed, nor cruel and unusual punishments inflicted.

Amendment IX
The enumeration in the Constitution, of certain rights, shall not be construed to deny or disparage others retained by the people.
Amendment X
The powers not delegated to the United States by the Constitution, nor prohibited by it to the States, are reserved to the States respectively, or to the people.

THE POWERS NOT DELEGATED TO THE UNITED STATES BY THE CONSTITUTION, ... ARE RESERVED TO THE STATES RESPECTIVELY, OR TO THE PEOPLE.

Too often we treat the states as if they are political subdivisions of the federal government. What we see in the Tenth Amendment is evidence that the exact opposite is true. We the People created the states, and through those states created the Constitution. The federal government is a creation of that Constitution, which places specific limits on its powers. The Tenth Amendment confirms that any power not specifically delegated to the federal government belongs either to the states, or if it is forbidden to the states, it remains with the people. Now imagine what life in America would be like if We the People actually enforced the Tenth Amendment on the federal government.

20.
THE VICE PRESIDENT

AMENDMENT XI
The Judicial power of the United States shall not be construed to extend to any suit in law or equity, commenced or prosecuted against one of the United States by Citizens of another State, or by Citizens or Subjects of any Foreign State.

AMENDMENT XII
The Electors shall meet in their respective states and vote by ballot for President and Vice President, one of whom, at least, shall not be an inhabitant of the same state with themselves; they shall name in their ballots the person voted for as President, and in distinct ballots the person voted for as Vice President, and they shall make distinct lists of all persons voted for as President, and of all persons voted for as Vice President, and of the number of votes for each, which lists they shall sign and certify, and transmit sealed to the seat of the government of the United States, directed to the President of the Senate; -- the President of the Senate shall, in the presence of the Senate and House of Representatives, open all the certificates and the votes shall then be counted; -- The person having the greatest number of votes for President, shall be the President, if such number be a majority of the whole number of Electors appointed; and if no person have such majority, then from the persons having the highest numbers not exceeding three on the list of those voted for as President, the House of Representatives shall choose immediately, by ballot, the President. But in choosing the President, the votes shall be taken by states, the representation from each state having one vote; a quorum

for this purpose shall consist of a member or members from two-thirds of the states, and a majority of all the states shall be necessary to a choice. [And if the House of Representatives shall not choose a President whenever the right of choice shall devolve upon them, before the fourth day of March next following, then the Vice President shall act as President, as in case of the death or other constitutional disability of the President. --] The person having the greatest number of votes as Vice President, shall be the Vice President, if such number be a majority of the whole number of Electors appointed, and if no person have a majority, then from the two highest numbers on the list, the Senate shall choose the Vice President; a quorum for the purpose shall consist of two-thirds of the whole number of Senators, and a majority of the whole number shall be necessary to a choice. But no person constitutionally ineligible to the office of President shall be eligible to that of Vice President of the United States.*

THE ELECTORS SHALL MEET IN THEIR RESPECTIVE STATES AND VOTE BY BALLOT FOR PRESIDENT AND VICE PRESIDENT

Originally, the Vice President was the first runner-up in the election for President. This caused problems for our second President, John Adams, when his Vice President, Thomas Jefferson, was from an opposing party. This was quickly changed with the Eleventh Amendment.

21.
SLAVERY

AMENDMENT XIII
Section 1.
Neither slavery nor involuntary servitude, except as a punishment for crime whereof the party shall have been duly convicted, shall exist within the United States, or any place subject to their jurisdiction.
Section 2.
Congress shall have power to enforce this article by appropriate legislation.
AMENDMENT XIV
Section 1.
All persons born or naturalized in the United States, and subject to the jurisdiction thereof, are citizens of the United States and of the State wherein they reside. No State shall make or enforce any law which shall abridge the privileges or immunities of citizens of the United States; nor shall any State deprive any person of life, liberty, or property, without due process of law; nor deny to any person within its jurisdiction the equal protection of the laws.
Section 2.
Representatives shall be apportioned among the several States according to their respective numbers, counting the whole number of persons in each State, excluding Indians not taxed. But when the right to vote at any election for the choice of electors for President and Vice President of the United States, Representatives in Congress, the Executive and Judicial officers of a State, or the members of the Legislature thereof, is denied to any of the male inhabitants of such State, being twenty-one years of age, and citizens of

the United States, or in any way abridged, except for participation in rebellion, or other crime, the basis of representation therein shall be reduced in the proportion which the number of such male citizens shall bear to the whole number of male citizens twenty-one years of age in such State.

NEITHER SLAVERY NOR INVOLUNTARY SERVITUDE,... SHALL EXIST WITHIN THE UNITED STATES

Slavery was not just a stain on the early republic, but on the world. While several colonies attempted to outlaw the slave trade while they were still British possessions, the king refused. As a compromise to get all thirteen states to ratify the Constitution, slavery was not outlawed, but the tools were put in place to allow it to "die on the vine". Sadly, it took almost "four score and seven years", not to mention the lives of many Americans, for slavery to finally be made illegal in the republic. And it would take another 100+ years for the effects of slavery on our institutions to be whittled away. Even worse, it seems millions of Americans today are still enslaved to the memories of the past. It is unfortunate we cannot outlaw the slavery of the mind the same way we did for slavery of the body.

22.
PUNISHING REBELLION

*Section 3.
No person shall be a Senator or Representative in Congress, or elector of President and Vice President, or hold any office, civil or military, under the United States, or under any State, who, having previously taken an oath, as a member of Congress, or as an officer of the United States, or as a member of any State legislature, or as an executive or judicial officer of any State, to support the Constitution of the United States, shall have engaged in insurrection or rebellion against the same, or given aid or comfort to the enemies thereof. But Congress may by a vote of two-thirds of each House, remove such disability.
Section 4.
The validity of the public debt of the United States, authorized by law, including debts incurred for payment of pensions and bounties for services in suppressing insurrection or rebellion, shall not be questioned. But neither the United States nor any State shall assume or pay any debt or obligation incurred in aid of insurrection or rebellion against the United States, or any claim for the loss or emancipation of any slave; but all such debts, obligations and claims shall be held illegal and void.
Section 5.
The Congress shall have the power to enforce, by appropriate legislation, the provisions of this article.*

SHALL HAVE ENGAGED IN INSURRECTION OR REBELLION AGAINST THE SAME, OR GIVEN AID OR COMFORT TO THE ENEMIES THEREOF

It seems rebellion must be punished. After the Confederate States lost the Civil War, there was still penance that had to be paid by those who engaged in rebellion. If someone had served the union, either in the military or government office, and then fought for the Confederacy, the Fourteenth Amendment made sure they would not be allowed to hold office again. That is, unless Congress voted to remove such a disability.

No one from the Civil War is still alive, so this section of the amendment may seem obsolete. However it is a reminder, not only of the dear price that was paid on both sides, but of the limitations of the human heart to forgive those who have hurt us.

23.
CHANGING THE UNION

A MENDMENT XV
Section 1.
The right of citizens of the United States to vote shall not be denied or abridged by the United States or by any State on account of race, color, or previous condition of servitude--
Section 2.
The Congress shall have the power to enforce this article by appropriate legislation.
AMENDMENT XVI
The Congress shall have power to lay and collect taxes on incomes, from whatever source derived, without apportionment among the several States, and without regard to any census or enumeration.
AMENDMENT XVII
The Senate of the United States shall be composed of two Senators from each State, elected by the people thereof, for six years; and each Senator shall have one vote. The electors in each State shall have the qualifications requisite for electors of the most numerous branch of the State legislatures.
When vacancies happen in the representation of any State in the Senate, the executive authority of such State shall issue writs of election to fill such vacancies: Provided, That the legislature of any State may empower the executive thereof to make temporary appointments until the people fill the vacancies by election as the legislature may direct.

This amendment shall not be so construed as to affect the election or term of any Senator chosen before it becomes valid as part of the Constitution.

THE CONGRESS SHALL HAVE POWER TO LAY AND COLLECT TAXES ON INCOMES

The Sixteenth and Seventeenth Amendments fundamentally changed the republic. Before 1913, unless you were in the military, the only regular contact you had with the federal government was the post office. After the Sixteenth Amendment was ratified, the government not only had the authority to legally tax your income, but a reason to be involved in every aspect of your life. Thanks to the avarice of early 20th Century Americans we now have to keep track of and report what we make, how we spend it, and even how we save our money and leave it to the next generation.

The other major change to the republic was the popular election of U.S. Senators. Originally, a state's legislature chose its senators. This made sense since the role of the U.S. Senate is for the states to have a voice in the federal government. However, by making a mountain out of a molehill, the states and their citizens were convinced it would be a good idea to relocate that power to the citizens rather than their representatives in their legislature. By removing the states from the process of making federal law, there was no one to object to the encroachment on states' rights. What we've seen since then is not only an ever expanding federal government, usurping the powers reserved to the states, but a wholesale change in how the republic is viewed. No longer do most Americans view themselves as citizens of a state that is united to others; instead they see themselves as citizens of the federal government and their states as anachronistic vestiges of the past.

24.
PROHIBITION

AMENDMENT XVIII
Section 1.
After one year from the ratification of this article the manufacture, sale, or transportation of intoxicating liquors within, the importation thereof into, or the exportation thereof from the United States and all territory subject to the jurisdiction thereof for beverage purposes is hereby prohibited.
Section 2.
The Congress and the several States shall have concurrent power to enforce this article by appropriate legislation.
Section 3.
This article shall be inoperative unless it shall have been ratified as an amendment to the Constitution by the legislatures of the several States, as provided in the Constitution, within seven years from the date of the submission hereof to the States by the Congress.
AMENDMENT XIX
The right of citizens of the United States to vote shall not be denied or abridged by the United States or by any State on account of sex.
Congress shall have power to enforce this article by appropriate legislation.

THE MANUFACTURE, SALE, OR TRANSPORTATION OF INTOXICATING LIQUORS ... FOR BEVERAGE PURPOSES IS HEREBY PROHIBITED.

We all know that prohibition was tried and then repealed. So why is it still in the Constitution? Because unlike many similar documents, the Constitution can only be added to. This not only gives us a written history of changes to the supreme law of the land, but the opportunity to learn from them.

For instance, consider the Eighteenth Amendment. In 1917 Americans still understood that for the United States government to do something, they must be delegated the power to do so in the Constitution. So when those who had spent decades trying and failing to get Americans to stop drinking could not get what they wanted through persuasion, they went to government intimidation. Although the Eighteenth Amendment did not prohibit the consumption of alcohol, it did severely restrict its manufacture, importation, and sale. It would take twenty-four years, the deaths of thousands, and the empowerment of organized crime for those in governments to realize you cannot change people's minds by simply passing a law or a constitutional amendment. Though it was repealed, the power this amendment gave to Washington, D.C. is still in effect today.

25.
SCHEDULING

A MENDMENT XX
Section 1.
The terms of the President and the Vice President
shall end at noon on the 20th day of January, and the terms
of Senators and Representatives at noon on the 3d day of
January, of the years in which such terms would have ended
if this article had not been ratified; and the terms of their
successors shall then begin.
Section 2.
The Congress shall assemble at least once in every year, and
such meeting shall begin at noon on the 3d day of January,
unless they shall by law appoint a different day.
Section 3.
If, at the time fixed for the beginning of the term of the
President, the President elect shall have died, the Vice
President elect shall become President. If a President shall
not have been chosen before the time fixed for the beginning
of his term, or if the President elect shall have failed to
qualify, then the Vice President elect shall act as President
until a President shall have qualified; and the Congress may
by law provide for the case wherein neither a President elect
nor a Vice President elect shall have qualified, declaring who
shall then act as President, or the manner in which one who
is to act shall be selected, and such person shall act
accordingly until a President or Vice President shall have
qualified.
Section 4.
The Congress may by law provide for the case of the death
of any of the persons from whom the House of

Representatives may choose a President whenever the right of choice shall have devolved upon them, and for the case of the death of any of the persons from whom the Senate may choose a Vice President whenever the right of choice shall have devolved upon them.
Section 5.
Sections 1 and 2 shall take effect on the 15th day of October following the ratification of this article.
Section 6.
This article shall be inoperative unless it shall have been ratified as an amendment to the Constitution by the legislatures of three-fourths of the several States within seven years from the date of its submission.

THE TERMS OF THE PRESIDENT AND THE VICE PRESIDENT SHALL END AT NOON ON THE 20TH DAY OF JANUARY

Modern society runs on calendars and schedules. When the republic started, Congress was required to meet only once a year, on the first Monday in December. The Twentieth Amendment moved that date, along with the starting date for the term of Congressmen, to January 3rd. It set the starting date for the Presidential and Vice Presidential terms to January 20th.

26.
TERM LIMITS

AMENDMENT XXI
Section 1.
The eighteenth article of amendment to the Constitution of the United States is hereby repealed.
Section 2.
The transportation or importation into any State, Territory, or possession of the United States for delivery or use therein of intoxicating liquors, in violation of the laws thereof, is hereby prohibited.
Section 3.
This article shall be inoperative unless it shall have been ratified as an amendment to the Constitution by conventions in the several States, as provided in the Constitution, within seven years from the date of the submission hereof to the States by the Congress.
AMENDMENT XXII
Section 1.
No person shall be elected to the office of the President more than twice, and no person who has held the office of President, or acted as President, for more than two years of a term to which some other person was elected President shall be elected to the office of the President more than once. But this Article shall not apply to any person holding the office of President when this Article was proposed by the Congress, and shall not prevent any person who may be holding the office of President, or acting as President, during the term within which this Article becomes operative from holding the office of President or acting as President during the remainder of such term.

NO PERSON SHALL BE ELECTED TO THE OFFICE OF THE PRESIDENT MORE THAN TWICE,

While it was tradition for a President of the United States to serve no more than two terms, there was no legal restriction for doing so until the passing of the Twenty-second Amendment in 1951. The reason for the amendment? Franklin D. Roosevelt had been elected for an unprecedented four terms, although he died shortly after beginning it. Those in the opposing party used the idea of term limiting the office of President as a campaign platform and won.

Although viewed as a restraint on the candidate, term limits are actually restrictions on the voters. F.D.R. won was elected President four times because a majority of the states voted for him that many times. Today, much as in the late 1940's, politicians and pundits are calling for term limits on other federal offices. Before we give them what they want, we should look closely and learn a lesson from the Twenty-first Amendment. The character of the person in office depends less on how long they serve, and more on how the electorate determines who to vote for.

27.
ELECTORS FOR D.C.

AMENDMENT XXIII
Section 1.
The District constituting the seat of Government of the United States shall appoint in such manner as the Congress may direct:
A number of electors of President and Vice President equal to the whole number of Senators and Representatives in Congress to which the District would be entitled if it were a State, but in no event more than the least populous State; they shall be in addition to those appointed by the States, but they shall be considered, for the purposes of the election of President and Vice President, to be electors appointed by a State; and they shall meet in the District and perform such duties as provided by the twelfth article of amendment.
Section 2.
The Congress shall have power to enforce this article by appropriate legislation.

A NUMBER OF ELECTORS ... EQUAL TO THE WHOLE NUMBER OF SENATORS AND REPRESENTATIVES IN CONGRESS TO WHICH THE DISTRICT WOULD BE ENTITLED IF IT WERE A STATE,

Over the years I have heard repeated calls for "D.C. statehood". However, Washington, D.C. is prohibited from being a state for a very good reason.

When our republic was created, the plan was for one or more states to voluntarily cede an area of ten square miles to be the seat of government for the union. Our founders did not want the nation's capital to be in any state. Why? Because they did not want a state, specifically a state government, to have legal authority over the nation's capital. So Article I, Section 8, Clause 17 of the Constitution gives sole legislative control of such a district to Congress. Since Washington, D.C. is not a state, it has no Congressmen. The House has allowed the district to elect two representatives, but they have no vote so they have no power.

The Twenty-third Amendment is a direct outcome of the lack of education about how the President of the United States is elected. Washington, D.C. is not a state, so it was not granted electors. Even the language of the amendment shows they are being granted electors equal to the number it would have if it were a state. So through this amendment, the other states have elevated the seat of government to the position of statehood for the purpose of electing a President.

Many people complain that the fact Washington, D.C. is not a state deprives them of representation. Remember, the purpose of D.C. is not to be a city, but the seat of a government. It was not created to have residents, or even businesses, except those of the federal government. Even those elected to federal office were not expected to live in the nation's capital, but only work there for a time. Those who live in the district do so, for the most part, voluntarily. Rather than making it a state, we should return Washington, D.C. to the federal district it was created for.

28.
POLL TAXES

AMENDMENT XXIV
Section 1.
The right of citizens of the United States to vote in any primary or other election for President or Vice President, for electors for President or Vice President, or for Senator or Representative in Congress, shall not be denied or abridged by the United States or any State by reason of failure to pay any poll tax or other tax.
Section 2.
The Congress shall have power to enforce this article by appropriate legislation.

THE RIGHT OF CITIZENS OF THE UNITED STATES TO VOTE ... SHALL NOT BE DENIED OR ABRIDGED BY THE UNITED STATES OR ANY STATE BY REASON OF FAILURE TO PAY ANY POLL TAX OR OTHER TAX,

While slavery may have been "dealt with" in the Thirteenth Amendment, that doesn't mean that racism was. Nearly a century after the Civil War, racism was still prevalent in parts of the country. A series of laws, known as Jim Crow Laws, were used to disenfranchise black and poor Americans. One of these laws was the poll tax.

A poll tax is any tax that must be paid in order to register to vote. The first state to implement a poll tax was Connecticut in 1649. Most state poll taxes were implemented in the 1860's-1890's, although Oklahoma instituted theirs in 1907. Several states repealed their poll taxes in the early 20th century, but by the ratification of the Twenty Fourth Amendment in 1964, five states still had them in place.

While most people focus on the poll tax, the Twenty Fourth Amendment prohibits the denial of the right to vote of any unpaid taxes. That means you cannot be denied the right to vote because you have not paid income, property, or any other taxes.

29.
REMOVAL OF A PRESIDENT

AMENDMENT XXV
Section 1.
In case of the removal of the President from office or of his death or resignation, the Vice President shall become President.
Section 2.
Whenever there is a vacancy in the office of the Vice President, the President shall nominate a Vice President who shall take office upon confirmation by a majority vote of both Houses of Congress.
Section 3.
Whenever the President transmits to the President pro tempore of the Senate and the Speaker of the House of Representatives his written declaration that he is unable to discharge the powers and duties of his office, and until he transmits to them a written declaration to the contrary, such powers and duties shall be discharged by the Vice President as Acting President.
Section 4.
Whenever the Vice President and a majority of either the principal officers of the executive departments or of such other body as Congress may by law provide, transmit to the President pro tempore of the Senate and the Speaker of the House of Representatives their written declaration that the President is unable to discharge the powers and duties of his office, the Vice President shall immediately assume the powers and duties of the office as Acting President. Thereafter, when the President transmits to the President pro tempore of the Senate and the Speaker of the House of

Representatives his written declaration that no inability exists, he shall resume the powers and duties of his office unless the Vice President and a majority of either the principal officers of the executive department or of such other body as Congress may by law provide, transmit within four days to the President pro tempore of the Senate and the Speaker of the House of Representatives their written declaration that the President is unable to discharge the powers and duties of his office. Thereupon Congress shall decide the issue, assembling within forty-eight hours for that purpose if not in session. If the Congress, within twenty-one days after receipt of the latter written declaration, or, if Congress is not in session, within twenty-one days after Congress is required to assemble, determines by two-thirds vote of both Houses that the President is unable to discharge the powers and duties of his office, the Vice President shall continue to discharge the same as Acting President; otherwise, the President shall resume the powers and duties of his office.

IN CASE OF THE REMOVAL OF THE PRESIDENT … THE VICE PRESIDENT SHALL BECOME PRESIDENT.

The only time the Twenty-fifth Amendment has been exercised is in the movies. However, as the pace of life has increased, the need to have a defined process for dealing with the death or incapacity of the President is needed. Contrary to what many say, a President's cabinet cannot remove him from office, but only temporarily transfer the power to act as President to the Vice President

30.
AN AMENDMENT AT LAST

AMENDMENT XXVI
Section 1.
The right of citizens of the United States, who are eighteen years of age or older, to vote shall not be denied or abridged by the United States or by any State on account of age.
Section 2.
The Congress shall have power to enforce this article by appropriate legislation.
AMENDMENT XXVII
No law, varying the compensation for the services of the Senators and Representatives, shall take effect, until an election of Representatives shall have intervened.

NO LAW, VARYING THE COMPENSATION FOR THE SERVICES OF THE SENATORS AND REPRESENTATIVES, SHALL TAKE EFFECT, UNTIL AN ELECTION OF REPRESENTATIVES SHALL HAVE INTERVENED.

Yes, the Bill of Rights are the first ten amendments to the Constitution. But did you know that the first Congress actually proposed 12 amendments?

The first amendment proposed would have allowed Congress to determine how many representatives would be in the House (something Congress has already done without constitutional authorization). This amendment was never ratified.

The second amendment proposed would have prevented the pay of Congress from changing until after a House election had taken place. This amendment was not ratified until 1992, when it became the Twenty-seventh Amendment.

31.
CONCLUSION

You've done it; you've read through the entire Constitution, including all the amendments, and the Declaration of Independence as well. Now what are you going to do? The John Jay quote before the prologue gives us a clue.

If you were diligent in your reading, you should know more of your rights than you did when you started. Knowing your rights is the first step in living as a free person. You have to know what your rights are if you're going to recognize when they are violated. Knowing where and how your rights are protected is how you prepare to defend and assert them. It's not good enough to claim you have free speech rights. Instead, what is the proper way to assert that? You may claim a right to be secure in your person, house, paper, and effects, but how do you go about defending that right? More importantly, how do you defend those rights for someone else? That's why Mr. Jay said we should not only be diligent in reading the Constitution, but in studying it as well. Reading tells you what rights are protected by the Constitution, but studying teaches you how to defend and assert them. That is not all Mr. Jay said in his quote though: We are to teach the rising generation to be free.

Sadly, very few of us were taught how to live free. You can either wallow in your deficiency or use your newfound knowledge to encourage us further. That is what John Jay's quote did for me. I saw it as a challenge, and it changed not only my life, but others' lives as well. Not only do I study the Constitution and teach others about it, but I make a point of teaching the next generation how to live free. That's the John

Jay Challenge: Not only to educate yourself, but to prepare those who will come after you. For how can we expect our children to live free if no one teaches them how?

Our generation does not live as free as previous ones, so don't leave this country even less free than the one we have today. To do that, I recommend you do two things.

First, do what you can. Not everyone is prepared to challenge city hall, file law suits, or protest in the streets. That's OK; do what you can. Just because you can't do something big and showy doesn't mean there's nothing you can do, and it certainly doesn't mean that what you do doesn't matter. So find something you can do and start doing it. Writing letters, teaching others, and supporting organizations all help. Trust me, even some kind words and emotional support can mean a lot. I spend a lot of time alone behind a computer, studying and researching, only to have people try to tear down what I'm doing. So when someone goes out of their way to encourage the work I'm doing, it makes a big difference.

Second, and probably the one we need to be reminded of the most, is to keep your eyes on where you want to be. In general, people have a tendency to focus on the problems rather than the solutions. Unfortunately, focusing on problems leads to frustration, depression, and isolation, which ultimately leads to inaction. By focusing on the goal, those who are on the journey with you bring encouragement, camaraderie, and the willingness to carry on.

You have taken a step toward restoring liberty for yourself, your family, and Americans everywhere. Now that you have taken one step, it's time to decide which step to take next. Take that step and join with those of us who are working to restore liberty in America. The journey will not be quick, and it will not be easy, but with a group of liberty loving patriots at your side, it will be a journey well worth taking. And you will have stories well worth telling your children and your grandchildren.

ABOUT THE AUTHOR

Author and speaker, Paul Engel has spent more than 20 years studying and teaching about both the Bible and the U.S. Constitution. That experience helps Paul explain difficult concepts in a way most people can understand. As one manager described, "Paul can take the most complex idea and explain it in a way my grandmother can understand." Freely admitting that he "learned more about our Constitution from School House Rock (a Saturday morning cartoon) than in 12 years of school" he says that anyone can be a constitutional scholar. Paul is available for speaking engagements and interviews. You can reach him at paul@constitutionstudy.com, and read more of his work at his website, (https://constituitonstudy.com)